Poems from a Tragic Comic

Surviving Cancer, Drinking, and Women

Dyann & Kayleigh, Thanks for making my job easy & fun!

David H. McGrath

Dave

PublishAmerica
Baltimore

First printing

At the specific preference of the author, PublishAmerica allowed this work to remain exactly as the author intended, verbatim, without editorial input.

ISBN: 1-4137-7525-X
PUBLISHED BY PUBLISHAMERICA, LLLP
www.publishamerica.com
Baltimore

Printed in the United States of America

DEDICATION:

For all the events and people that have come into my life and challenged me, hurt me, loved me, made me stronger, and made me learn…especially: my family, Crohn's, cancer, alcohol, my students, my friends, my teachers, and all the flavory girls

ACKNOWLEDGEMENTS:

Special thanks to my parents Paul and Mary Beth, my siblings Jon, Carolyn, Tom, and Meg, Auntie, Uncle Charley, Katie, and Matt, Gram and Grandpa Dave, Aunt Carol, Grandpa Paul and Grandma Tommie, Jen McGrath, Brendan, Conor, and Colleen, The Gassers

My friends: Andy Marshall (a.k.a. Dr. Marshall), Matt Vautour (a.k.a. MTV), Patrick Salmon (a.k.a. Mod 40A's 7th man), Andrew Bartkus (a.k.a. Drew, a.k.a. Drewster, a.k.a. Newton), Carl Brugnoli (a.k.a. Crazy Carl, a.k.a. Law Talking Guy), Elizabeth Rice, Glen (yeah, I played with U2) Goland, Mike Fallon, Suzie Cassidy, John Higgins (a.k.a. Higgins), Joanne Kostopoulos, Scott (let's go Islanders!) Seremet, Tim St.Louis, Alisa Brugnoli, Ellie Springer, Hilary Sahn, The 32 Ruggles Crew: Cailin, Ian, Wiper, Terry, Adam, Tyler (The Dude), Becca, Katie, Rita

All the flavory girls (whom without there would be a lot less poetry): Leanne D., Meghan M., Julia G., Maura D., Judy C., Wendy D., Kristen G., Lauren S., Elizabeth, Anne, Ami T., Julie D., Karen L., Jenn A., Heather W., Carolyn O', Katherine D., Katie K., Mel S.
Dr. Schwenn and all the doctors and nurses that helped me at UMass hospital, Worcester, MA
The Boston College Police Department
The Westborough News, WAAF
Karen Baumgartner, Deb Williamson-McCabe, Gale Levine, Jen Annesi, Yahnique Robb, Sue Augusto, and Roberta Russo

People that have inspired me: My family, Justin Horton, Danny Manning Jr., Sandy Shoro, Cam Neely, Denis Leary, Kevin Smith, Michael Moore, Jon Stewart, Oprah Winfrey, Dave Letterman, the Beatles, Extreme, Pearl Jam, Great Big Sea, Old Brown's Daughter, Focusin (www.focusinmusic.com), The 2001 BC Hockey Team, The 2004 Red Sox, all the flavory girls

"I'M A HAPLESS ROMANTIC ST-T-TUTTERING P-POET JUST CALL ME A TRAGIC COMIC CAUSE I'M, IN, IN LOVE WITH YOU"

Tragic Comic, Extreme

Stylus

127 McElroy Commons
Boston College
Chestnut Hill, MA 02167

Date: November 8, 1993

Dear David McGrath

Re: Name of Submission:_____

We are sorry to inform you that your submission has not been accepted for publication in Stylus. A majority of our staff did not feel that it was ready for publication. We would like to remind you that all works are judged anonymously, and are voted on only after a thorough discussion.

Please do not be discouraged or deterred by this setback. It is very difficult to determine what few pieces we are able to publish, as we receive many diverse works of literature and art. Also, it is common practice for literature to be revised. If you would like to review the comments that were made about your submission, please contact a member of the Editoral Board. We welcome revisions and are eager to watch the progress of works. Please continue to submit to Stylus, as we appreciate your contributions.

We appreciate the time and effort that you have spent submitting your piece to Stylus. If you have any questions or comments about you piece or Stylus in general, please do not hesitate to contact the staff in the Stylus office, or at extension 3506. Thank you for your continued support.

Sincerely,

Stylus Editorial Board

Stylus
Boston College
McElroy 127
Chestnut Hill, MA 02167

Date: 4/6/94

Dear David,

We regret that your submission(s) has not been selected for publication in the spring issue of *Stylus*. This in no way reflects disinterest in your work. We would be delighted to consider any future pieces that you wish to submit, including revisions. All submissions are considered with careful attention and under artist/author anonymity. We would be happy to answer any questions you may have or to discuss the review that your piece received. You can contact us at 552-3506 or in McElroy 127.

Thank you for the time you took in submitting to *Stylus*. The creative power of artists and students like you is what makes *Stylus* a reality. Please consider submitting again for the spring issue.

Sincerely,

The Editorial Board

Contents

Unwanted

Trying to wish away
Unplanned traces
On the page,
Curse the cursive
I can't control.
Unwanted swirls
Of my world,
Words of
The flavory girls.
Hurt dominates
Happy here,
Cynical seepings contaminate
Fresh water.
Cleanse me of
My sins of intensity,
Soul escaping and severity,
Such beauty I feel
I must report,
Emotions that set myself up to
Drown before the ink even dries,
Consequences I keep seeing
Yet I keep believing
That anything short of this
Wouldn't be me,
Like what I write,
Unwanted.

Assignment: V-Day Massacre

My essence percolates knowing I'm wasting time
Writing words of you- you, my mega-nemesis,
A constant reminder of my perpetually cursed life.
My laser eyes attempt to burn gaping holes in your
Pathetic existence, as I make it my vocation to
Drag you down with me.
Face to face, it takes every calming technique,
Every anger management skill, every reminder of
Consequence for me not to puncture your throat.
You can't hide the deception in your eyes,
All the lies you drop on me so effortlessly,
So habitually. Your fakeness oozes out of your
Every pore like an acid invading my every nerve.
An unbeauty of crackling weeds, a growing hatred
That makes me want to invent new expressions of
Disgust- like your cure for laughs, your chemo
For joy, your pill for caring.
Regret of both past and present showers upon me,
My wish of a youless future remains an unmovable
Faint star. You purge happiness from me, as I try
To swallow the vomit in my mouth- I expel in the
Water, this extra salty sea of gloom you create around me.
The reflection I see on the surface shows reminding
Wrinkles of that Black Christmas Night, a meeting
That led to this miserable misery, this new definition
Of vicious disdain, this cynical hate cancer with the
Poorest of a poor prognosis.
I cannot, I will not give you anymore time or effort
Of my verse and leave you with my thoughts of your
Extirpation, writhing alone in a cold wet basement.

Vacuum

Slowly sucking,
I feel space dividing
Between my call and the answer.
A black hole realization
That I'm drifting alone
In an all too familiar galaxy of miscalculation.
This near discovery
Seemed so close, so real
But this pull tells me to let go,
To fall into this self-created abyss.
I can't even tell which way I'm facing
As I float in my torn paper space suit.
I see Venus out of the corner of my eye,
Her orbit is taking her away
Regardless of my rocket's navigation,
Yet I still stare at Her,
Sometimes so bright,
I still want to
Make it to the surface,
But it's always night up here.
I keep telling myself
All this space dementia
Will be worth it, all the voices will
Eventually calm and a
New Sun will be born,
A calm clear presence in the sky
That will give meaning to me.
I can't deny the facts,
The numbers, the message
My computer gives me
Through if, thens, and whys

But I keep typing,
Trying to find the formula,
The equation that I'm
Hoping someday will
Take me to Her, my Venus.
Can I reverse this vacuum?

Peel

My skin,
Touch my skin,
Feel the layers
As you peel them away.
You are the only one
I allow inside,
My fruit is yours
To taste and devour.
I know it may not be
The right time of year,
But it's ripe for the pleasing.
My sweet inside,
Dip it in your favorite sauce,
Your sticky sugar juice.
Take me in your mouth
And guide my stems down,
On the ground we'll roll.
Let nature take us,
Make our cores touch,
Our vines embrace.
We will replenish,
Bask, bloom,
Not rot in this heat.

Gum

Sweetly and seductively
Tongue tie the stick
In your mouth.
Watch your teeth
As you copingly chew,
Mesh the flesh
With the sugary juice.
Blow bubbles 'til
It pops,
Keep going,
Eyes spin like tops.
Feel the rush
Your lips will
Soon feel beyond enough,
Unwrapped and wanting
And tell me this
Is the stuff.

Desert

I will walk away.
Sitting in the middle,
I try to vaguely
Center in.
As I pull towards the left,
I see the ship in the distance.
My humor is stolen,
The smile is not mine.
I'm at the dry right,
Trying to make anything
River into laughter,
But the pair of mouths
Are emptying the fresh start away.
I will walk away.
I consciously try to imagine
This drought isn't bothering me,
Knowing each oasis
May seep into the sand.
Is it the same?
Is it a game of survival?
I will walk away.
Will footprints follow me into the ocean?
Should I cover my tracks or light a signal fire?
Will I watch these two disappear into the golden moon?
Will a triangle reform?
A three pointed star of footprints?
Deserted in the desert
With these questions,
I will walk away.

What She Is

First time I felt her,
I knew she was trouble.
Without my knowing,
She was under my skin,
I was seeing double with
Her literally on my mind.
My brain hurt so much,
Thinking about her all the time.
She grew on me so, so fast.
Out of control,
I needed drugs to stop this.
Alcohol, cocaine, even LSD
Not strong enough to
Get her off my brain.
VP16, carboplatinum, and bleomycin,
Dr. Love's orders to rid me of this-
A case of infatuation so strong,
I lost my hair over her.
An obsession so rooted,
She owned part of my mind.
A great deal of help from my friends
And the drugs did the trick.
I pray she'll never be back...
...she won't.
She can strike anyone at anytime because
Of what she is:
Is anything but benign.
Even though she's gone
For good, I will never forget her
And the lessons she taught me.

You're In

The blackest of black,
My cold center.
You're my whole summer...
The sun, the light.

You reach me,
My core like Pluto.
So far away,
But I still feel your warmth.

Through my protective atmosphere
I let your rays in.
The other stars try,
But you're the brightest to me.

I'm jealous of Mercury's position,
But I don't think he appreciates you
Like I do,
Cherishing each sunrise.

You're in,
My deepest layer.
I just wonder,
Is my reflection reaching?

Boston Bar Scene

Music blaring,
Another song I don't know.
I see the door open,
The bouncer checks her ID
As the lonely winter air seeps in.
She looks like you
In the shadow,
I'm taken there
To our meeting, the feeling.
My temporary suspension of disbelief gets me,
I forget what city I'm in.
This Boston bar scene
Isn't doing it for me anymore,
I'm wondering if it will ever change.
The same people having the same
Conversations,
I really wanted her to be you.

Metaphorical and physical
Rain reign
Slips sullenly on
My face.
An embrace
Is the Sun
Here among
Clinical afternoon slumber.
Nuclear rays
Knocking on my windowpane,
My anti-pain,
Clear moment awakening
To this sudden Empire
Of Grey.
Please display
What's underneath
This cold humidity,
Come to me
As nature intends,
Shine through and
Let your vision bend
This light,
You are a prism
In the night,
Please beat these clouds
Like I know you can…

Everything but Close

She says all the right words,
She always does the right things.
She knows how to make me laugh,
She makes me care again.

She's everything I want,
Yeah, everything I'm looking for.
She's everything I want to be,
Yet she's everything but close to me.

She has the eyes and the smile,
Just the right personality.
She takes me to these places,
And that's where I want to be.

I know we have this connection,
Some thing we can work out.
This so-called distance hang up is killing me,
She says it gives her doubt.

She's everything I want,
Yeah, everything I'm looking for.
She's everything I want to be,
Yet she's everything but close to me.

I know she doesn't feel the same,
I guess I'll have to deal,
The fact that she's everything, and she's there.
I feel like nothing, when I tell her I'm here...

For her, and I tell her two is the magic number,
Two, two, and two,
But I'm left as one,
Alone in this state.

She's everything I want,
Yeah, everything I'm looking for.
She's everything I want to be,
Yet she's everything but close to me.

Great Scott's

I never thought I
Could enjoy the dance floor like I
Did:
Staring into her eyes,
Like we were the only ones there.
It was a year later,
But the opposite feeling.
I cut the rug with happiness this time,
Sneaking in a few kisses
While I could.
I felt comfortable,
I felt home,
I held on.

Garden State

Take me to
Your garden state,
Waste me with a kiss
In the rain
So hard the Sun comes out,
Live the moment
With your dripping wet mind
And don't rewrite the ending.
Own the moment,
Come down off
Your tightrope
Of really feeling
And spread immediate change.
Get in it now,
All green and growing,
Roll around in Life
And plant yourself.
Write a song
Proclaiming yourself
And infect the earth
With your
Garden state.

Lost and Found

Lost,
A glance turns towards
Your blue oceans.
They hypnotize me
And my world is yours.
Caught in the natural current,
I drown
In your startling beauty.

Found,
This new world,
A warm connection that
I long to keep close.
I see the reflection
In your sky iris,
My smile that
You created,
Sparks that can't be denied.

Lost and found
As I stare,
Wondering if you feel
Even a fraction of this.

Memory Tree

I know somewhere
Carved in my memory tree
Is a vision of our love
A symbol that will always be there.

Even though a ring
Was not added while we were together
The tree's bark is still strong.

Sometimes I look at the words I etched
For you, I know I meant them all-
The feelings were that strong.

Sometimes in my mind
I'm walking in the woods,
My heart always leads me to the heart
I drew on our tree.

I try to embrace my memory tree
But it's not the same, it's not really there.
Yet, I still have that vision,
I still have that feeling.

Miss K.

Miss K.,
I have a big crush in you.
I'm sitting in the back of the class,
But it still is obvious.
I frantically wave my hand
Trying to get your attention,
Wondering why you won't call on me,
Give me a chance to answer.
Miss K.,
No one I know is quite like you,
You know about Jedi mind tricks
And hat tricks.
I wish I could be closer to you,
But in the back row I admire you
From afar,
Is your desk too far away to notice me?

Sand 360's

Sandy circles,
Shadows in the middle,
Letting the starlight in.
How the sun creates magnetic heat
With the beautiful sand.
The wish of walking,
Sinking my feet in the following grains.
Deeper in the shadows I stare,
Finding out what controls
The tides, temperatures, clouds,
These sight-circles
That distort, fake with play.
But off the parquet, the sands speak to me,
I feel their truth.
In subtleties I figure no quicksand,
Rather a sturdy beach.
Praying that the beach returns
My feelings,
I believe these sandy circles might.

Shirundo

I look up to see you,
Your wings take me
Temporarily away from
This cynical nest I've made.
My eyes breathe happiness
When I look at you,
I want to hold you
And nestle in your
Comfortable feathers.
I know we dove off that
Cliff together,
Not knowing what was below.
I'll hold onto you,
Shirundo,
Knowing we can glide together
And find the ideal
Landing spot.

Sad Deathnight!

Sad death night tonight,
A call not returned
And the flowers withered
As death took over.
In three days, the actual night.
It's over,
My only wish won't be,
But just left burning in the wax.
Death lives on
Through poetic injustices,
And all time sacrificed
Becomes wasted.
One more,
And I'll do it again,
To make ten
And nine will be it,
With the sad death night.
The actual night,
Hints of celebration there
And here, merely barely.
Surprise took over
And the hopes were shattered,
But, with even thoughs
And specks of smiles
Not as euphoric as if
Actual presence,
The voice was heard
And the call was returned
On this sad death night.
A heart

Injected with the small hope
That still remains tonight,
Wondering why I thanked
For the call of hope?
The feelings were there,
While still here tonight,
The cold blue fire
A little more yellow, but still green
On this sad deathnight.

Sadder, Deader, Darker (Sad Deathnight! II)

My success is my failure,
She never will reveal (never should).
I pushed the small candle,
Gave it the needed nudge
Over the cliff,
And death's ocean engulfed it.
It's a score of years now,
But an argument for a mercy rule.
The object changed,
The feeling remained.
The wax,
Now in my ears
Has built up so,
Hope needs to burn it,
A hope that is hidden.
Somewhere, I don't know where,
I see her
Bearing gifts in the death.
The red roses,
Again have been sadly poisoned.
And the fire heart,
It has spread to the stone marker of death.
In the recipe,
Now far beyond tradition
And yet so simple.
My lungs wish on it,
But the smoke inhibits blowing
As I send the final message.
Presents, presence, presents, presence?
A question,
What would rather be?
Hours, days with death,
A black crawling cancer

Whose seed was sown so many years ago.
Will I reach my next,
Or has She won?
The Doctor has the medicine
To birth the day
Of the happy cure.
"Will the anniversary
Remain black?" I ask

Timing

I was driving home alone tonight,
Thinking of you.
I pictured you sitting there next to me,
Like you did those few times.
I wanted you to be there
I wondered if it would happen again.
I was taken back to November
When I somehow knew the page.
I cherish those little glimpses I saw of you,
They're dear to my heart to this day.
My thoughts of you distracted my driving,
As gazing into your eyes used to do.
I thought of the timing and how bad it was,
Cursing Fate under my breath.
I was remembering the last time you sat there
In my parked car saying goodbye.
I was driving home alone tonight,
Thinking of the next time you would be
Sitting there saying hi.

Yawkey Way

Gate A,
You're my companion as I
Wait before the game.
It seems they were only selling
Tickets in pairs
As I see all the happy couples walk by.
My front row seat
Only temporarily takes away
From my jealousy-
I instinctively ask God
Why my hand is empty.
Then I realize,
I already know who I want
Sitting next to me.
Even in the last row of the bleachers
On the rainiest day,
I've already met her...
...And it doesn't matter what hat she wears.

Winks Across a Room

Winks across a crowded room,
Subtle gestures that connect us
In a crowd.
Temporarily, we are the only
Ones there,
Sharing what no one else knows.
Amidst the banter we find
A peaceful embrace in our minds,
Feeling each other in a way
Only imaginable to most.
We create just a simple smile,
Yet it means so much
When we wink across a room.

Flood

I'll never forget when you first washed up on shore,
That border seemed so foreign to me.
You said you knew the extreme,
And my immediate bias made the first,
A bad impression that would quickly
Go with the Fall leaves. And, with the later leaves,
The beach was left barren.
The flood first hit, but we all would miss it,
Still creating it in our eyes.
A closeness that pushes the water on the sand.
Our memories everyday etched in the tan concrete,
To be reflected upon each time the moon hit
The blue valleys. Walking away,
I dug my own canyon,
Flooding it too often,
My tree's veins couldn't cope.
Each branch that was intact was
Slowly melting in the poison ashes.
But you, you flooded me with your
Fresh air.
I tried to take it in, but couldn't.
I'd always deny the destruction, not caring for the people it affected.
A summer in the woods, I learned the botanical roots,
I learned what to use and how much,
Making the prefect bonsai tree.
I wanted to tell you,
Show you how proud I was.
But the day you didn't wash up onto my new shore,
I cried a flood in my plant's sod.
I understood, but still filled the empty cavern
With regretful blue reflection.
But the day, that day I wrote this all down was the day.
With that one report of the atmosphere
The whole earth seemed a temperate forest.
The rain had just began, and I cried a flood of joy.

Everlasting Gobstopper

When I leave the store
My sweet candy
I caress you,
Swirling you around my tongue.
My sweet social sphere,
I'm laughing as more honey is poured.
I crave more,
Hurrying to peel away each layer of my
Candy coat.
The friendly surfaces disappear quickly,
Each one faster than the last.
The bitter brown sugar tastes like water now,
And my core is reached.
The confection is gone
As I bite my tongue
And hit the harsh kernel.
I can't control my words at this point,
My sour center
Spills blood and tears.
As I pathetically return to the candy store,
My sugar-high vision is so blurred
I disregard all the signs that say stop.
You see,
Everlasting Gobstoppers are not for everyone.

Off-Guard

I rang the phone
Through her ear,
But I couldn't pick up
The thoughts I wanted.
She silently said
She was busy,
But still decided to hold on.
I let the red river
Gush from my mouth,
And it was emptying
Into her pool of laughter.
I dove in with the question,
One she had said yes to before.
But this time,
She said before was a "yes"
Of being off guard.
She forgot to tell me
She was permanently on the other line.
She forgot,
And suddenly she was
Too busy.

Fingertips

She's on the fingertips of my mind,
The borderline of my soul.
I felt too much too early,
And my prints have been erased
From her person.
Only glances now,
We cannot see the windows inside.
The ground becomes eyes
With each approach,
And my fingertips wipe the sweat.
It trickles down to my
Beating throat,
As I try to shove my heart back down.
Every time, it's an attack,
I'm paralyzed to the ground.
The concrete thought
Is a train hitting my body,
I'm lying flat.
I reach out,
Trying to pull myself up.
By now,
It's only my fingertips
Sifting through
The ashes of hope.
My fingertips,
That could be caressing her.

I sub-let my thoughts
Until the room is empty.
A neon sign is left
And it screams 80's to me.
A breeze invades my brain,
Uninvited, it turns tornado.
I remember the spinning,
But the mattress is dry now.
Falling back on feathers
Climbing the wall with my worn down nails,
I reach and regulate
The fire that was out of control.
Everything settles,
The lights go on
And I am surrounded.
They were here all the time,
Lost in the dark shadows
Of my selfishness.

708ZEI (Little Red Car)

Festiva,
Because of you
I will never forget.
It was the last time I saw you,
You peeled away without hesitation,
I was dirt on the closed avenue.
Now, just imagining your curves
Makes me see the red
That kissed the wind.
Everywhere I look,
My confusion sees you,
You downshift me with
The 50/50 memories,
Every smile tastes salty.
The flooded streets make me wonder,
Why did you run me over?
Are the rules of the road
Different in Jersey?
I tried my key-ring,
Not knowing you had a private mechanic.
A mechanic whose hands now
Caress and hold your hood up,
While I lay down on Bowman Street.
It's too late,
The fire in the ignition has started,
The key turned.
And even though I still see
These imitation little red cars,
If one of them happens to be you,
I will have to turn my head and let you drive
Away, by, and goodbye.

History Class Rush Hour (For 50 minutes)

I
Drive
Into the
Bottleneck,
Until the pressure
Stops me. Waiting, I
Give a subtle 360. Very
Few acquaintances in this sea
Of cars. As the heat throbs down,
I ask if it will be a sunny day. But,
In the rearview mirror, I see the familiar
Model. I've seen the car before, such a perfect
Body and year. Only sporadic glances, not to re-
Veal the stare. Do my sides lie, or is it closer than
It appears? I know of the aerodynamics, still wonder
Of the engine. In the rush hour, I wish I was the model
Mechanic. In the rush hour, I always break down. I push my
Poor excuse to the side and let the others pass as I look down.

Black Indifference of Immortality

In the black indifference of immortality
I find myself.
Lost, I find myself.
I search space not caring,
I know it will never end.
I blame myself for the vicious path I've taken,
It's circumference
Circles my mind,
Tightening the noose.
I can't see in this room,
The Blackness of Death has surrounded me.
She seduces me,
Even though I know what she means.
She's forever. Her eyes tell me
The pain will be over,
Immortality is forever.
I feel a door
On this ledge I've now climbed.
The knob frightens me,
Being so close to what I don't know.
She says under her breath to open it,
Everything will be okay,
I feel the lie in her voice.
Her forms talks, she screams silence.
I can't stay away from her,
The black indifference of her mind
Has trapped me.

What I feel,
Not to be kept in.
What my eyes tell me,
No comparison to:
Your face of a phenomenology.
Such a celestial smile,
It's always the smile.
My heart aches.
A few lines to simply say
You are beautiful.

KEG

A subconscious want
That was released.
I make my way to the kitchen,
Wanting to tap into
The source of the sort of
Buzzing in my head.
It doesn't matter if it is cheap or imported,
I will have brewing feelings inside.
I want to squeeze out
Every last tempting ounce
From the silver lining.
My past haunts rise to my memory,
And as I sip, I recall
A time when she may have been mine.
When the claddagh could not open
This barrel of intoxicating opportunity,
It was put on the wrong way,
Leaving me drunk but dry
With an empty plastic cup.

C O'C

I reach for you,
My sweet monogram
Wiping my eyes clean,
Your smell brings me back
To the first time I laid my
Eyes upon you.
You soaked up my nervous
Sweat as I hoped for the best.
You cleansed me of all
The build-up covering my
Soul's epidermis,
The stains of broken dreams
Tattooed on my chest.
Showering your love
Upon me,
You make it easier
For me to take off my hat
And get soaked.
I long to touch
You as my naked body gets
Drenched with a sprinkle
Of your care.
I step out and hold you
Against me,
Thankful for the morning.

A.M.

If only I had set my alarm,
You woke me so suddenly.
A sight and sound I didn't know before
Because I was craving the dark.
You tempt me with your sun
And we flirt with each other,
As the moon and sun dance together,
Touching only the way they can.
Nature's watch ticking away
Graduation to a seasoned time bomb.
Turning the hands ahead,
I see more light with the A.M.
Light stretching from New Jersey
To Prince Edward Island.
In the city,
Gilbert waits for the light.
Anticipating the A.M. horizon,
The dawn warmth coming,
Making the night seem so far away.

M.D.

The doctor is in,
And so am I.
She could cure any
Ailment that might befall me.
But, it seems she's sick too...
Of me.
She could prescribe
The real medicine I need
To antidote the poison bottles
I have been self-medicating with.
I'd never eat an apple a day
Just to see, M.D.
Dr. Feelgood,
She's in the top five
Of them all.

Oceans

Her eyes of the ocean
Reflecting a sky blue.
Filled with unknown sees
Of discoveries.
Deep, deeper, deepest,
Lost in their depth.
The warm ocean,
It surrounds me.
I call to her,
Only bubbles.
With this sea of water
I see my sea of oceans.
The waves of emotions
Seen in her eyes of the oceans.
What I hear in the sea shell
Is yet to be.

The Mighty J.V. (for Jack Vigliatura)

We stand in doubt,
At half mast for the flag boy,
Not knowing what to do, say, or think.
When I come face to face with Fate
What should I ask?
How could you take the sun?
How could you steal this light?
And what are we to say?
I can only hear the echo of a lost voice,
The static of an unknown frequency.
He's singing of his future,
By the grace of God he went-
Great or grave unknown.
And, what are we to do?
Thoughts come to me of
What could have been.
Why did Destiny take from us
This success waiting to happen?
And, what are we to think?
I challenge defenseless Destiny
With my barrage of questions,
But I get no answer.
Questions remain,
A circle of thoughts with no reason or answer.
Asking why did this happen?
Why, why, why?
And, what are we to do?
I wish I had known you, she said we would have been best friends...

The Word

The word I see in your face,
The word I see in your eyes,
The word I see in your smile,
The word I see in your voice.
The word I see when
I see you is beauty.
The word I see is
What you are:
Beautiful.

Mistaken

The skies were blinded
By the emerald I thought was
In her eyes.
Maybe it changed
In my mind somehow,
But the beauty remained.
Blinded was I,
Light blue is her true color,
The sky never ending,
And into this beauty
I could stare forever.

Standing in Silence

I will not deny this jealousy,
She in one of my best friends.
My anger is etched in the sand
When the tide comes in,
And I look for her in the sea-
Weed I placed out. Walking down the aisle
Of the beach,
The under-toe invites me.
A life in the water, maybe,
I think,
But I'm wearing
My very best clothes.
She screams sirens to me,
I reach for the nearest shell
To hear my future.
It's diamond-like reality
Cuts and corrupts my defenses,
And I violently drop the conch
To find I'm suddenly
Knee deep.

Life's Ocean

In life's ocean,
Those on the beach
Envy those deep in the water.
Those deep in the water
Take for granted that they won't drown.
Those wading are caught in uncertainty,
Not knowing whether to retreat or dive.
Maybe we should all dive in and swim around
Until we find a depth that isn't too shallow
Or far from the shore,
And a style that isn't too difficult or free.

Hayes-McGrath
(to my family on St. Patrick's Day)

With the seventeenth approaching
I feel my green blood flowing.
As I listen to "And the Band Played Waltzing Matilda"
I recall relatives singing
Of a war and time I don't know.
The notes fill me with the Passion o' the Irish,
A passion of both love and temper
Like Irish history itself:
Plagued by hardships,
Helped by faith.
A tradition I am now part of
As I sing "Sunday Bloody Sunday".
My Irish blessing:
That I have been going through life
Carrying with me
The names and clan
Hayes-McGrath.

Foreign Language

Now five years escaped from my soul,
I read words that are my heart on paper,
Proof I gave to you of my Love.

They take me back to
A feeling I've slowly forgotten,
A place where I feel more complete.

So far away now, when I could
Recite those words – they were
A special language we shared.

A surrealism surrounds me
As I try to decipher
The feelings expressed by these words.

This foreign language
Reveals a distant emotion,
A gap self-filled by murky salt water.

I'd still dive blind for you,
For even the slightest chance
Of being able to understand that foreign language again.

A page of the feelings held in my heart
My thoughts of you, as numerous as the stars.
Upon these stars I make a wish,
Hoping none fall.
Wondering and knowing:
Knowing how I love your smile,
It's always the smile,
A thing of beauty.
A picture of this smile I try to hold
In my memory forever.
An angel from the city of angels.
Just to hear your voice, I see a rose,
I'm away.
But when I see you, you are music to my eyes,
A whole symphony.
I'm drunk,
With happiness – a feeling that's hard to express in words.
It makes the time I don't see you seem like forever.
Wondering:
Is there a chance?
Is Cupid dead?
Will everyone's hearts remain unopened?
Why does it feel like forever?
What I know and wonder.
First thing I think when I wake, last before I sleep.
One of the many pages,
Not sweetness, but the truth
Written straight from my heart.

Through

The darkness
Was creeping all over
Her eyes still shown
Through the dusk
Fell at the time
I saw her
Pretty face
The facts I did
Not know her
Effect on
To the truth
Fullness of beauty
Full of her
Sky eyes of pretty
Nestling celestialness of
Course sing through thoughts
That always occupy
Eyed her fullness
In the darkness
She shown through.

In Defense of Bill (written in 1995)

I remember,
I was only twelve but
The pain feels like today.
They all blame Bill for the pain,
Selecting their memories
Like Fenway condiments
On a dog.
A life recalled by one second,
None of it was fair.
1918 was so long ago...

86

It all ended,
A relationship that started at Fenway Park,
A six-year-old became the Coca-Cola kid
And Yaz hit one out.
My summer Love almost made complete in 86,
But burned a memory so harsh,
I only saw the ball go through once,
Turning my head for each painful replay.
88, 90, 95, 99...
And then 2003:
Game 7 at the Stadium
Is all I have to say,
A new pain that challenged 86.
A play I never saw as I got into
My car during the bottom of the eighth.
Enter a savior in center field
And a prophet from Arizona...
July, 2004, 10 1/2 behind,
A nation was told to keep the faith.
A post-season birth,
An Anaheim sweep,
A new hero named Papi.
Down 0-3,
Best come back ever...I could look at the look
On Jeter and A-Rods faces forever.
Swept the Series...
All the pain gone in that final underhand toss...it was all worth it,
Yes, they really did it.

9/18/00

And there I was
Lying next to Fate in her bed
I wanted to tell her,
Talk to Fate about the choices.
I couldn't,
A feeling told me the results
Might twist her
The wrong way.
I laid there silent
Wanting to wrap myself in
Her every breath.
Flirtatious Fate,
How can I tell her
Without knowing what she knows?
I innocently
Held her hand for a moment,
A subtle silent hint.
There I was,
And I let go.

Twinkle

If really these
Are what count,
Look up at a
Clear night sky,
Across borders and
Plains and
Atmospheric reigns
Runs the shooting silvery
Trail of my limitless
For you.
Unconditionally out
Of control,
Lay back and the sky
Will show,
The unbelievable
Every twinkle
Can add up to...

It Was a Good Run

Five years,
I'm ready to go back on my word
Let her back in my life
I know she'll hurt me again,
But I need the release...
I need to feel her on my lips
Swallow her burning sensation.
I welcome her pain,
It makes me forget.
I get to become someone
Other than myself with her,
She's my excuse.
I fall back in Love with her
And alienate all who care about me.

Without You With You

Without you with you
I find myself
Lying down in my imagination
Separate togetherness tonight,
We look at that same moon
We did last night.
I hope tomorrow
We can hold hands in the
Reflection as we did before,
Let the tide take us there.

Mix

I want to make her the
Perfect mix,
She won't skip
Any songs when she listens.
I want to make the perfect mix-for her
Fast, slow – she'll listen
To it every day
I want her to take this
CD everywhere- make
It a permanent fixture-
A sturdy juke-box, and
All her songs come up
In a perfect row.

Border Café

Talking,
Smiling, sharing.
It was a good night,
One where I temporarily
Put my worry on hold.
Joking,
Being happy,
Living life,
Just everything-
And just as I thought it
Might not get any better,
I felt you grab me.

Skittish

This word,
It's one of the things I like about you
The fact that I needed a dictionary and you didn't.
Yet, it goes beyond that.
I want to take you "beyond skittish",
For each new word you give me,
I'll take you to an unknown place.
Even to me, as I write these words
Skittish seems so calm, so certain.
I want my arms wrapped around you
To make you un-skittish,
Our thoughts to focus on the
Candle-music moment,
Letting our hearts rule our minds.

Confetti Hope

And what happened to last week?
My new alcohol,
There's something I'm missing in the mix
About her and what it meant.
She invited me,
Asked me to stay,
Put her to bed,
Fell asleep to my voice.
"Can I call you back in 20 minutes?",
she said...last week.
Too dumb to get the point,
To low to say I forget,
I deny my feelings.
My confetti hope,
Seeps through my fingers,
Confetti hope
Ashes in my eye.

Dreams

My dream,
I miss you famously
Like how many stars on a
Late August night
In Prince Edward Island,
A single dot in
Our Milky Way of sharing.
A need, not want
To look at the same sky,
Sleep until whenever
To get up and create
New constellations of art.
Run away to the acres
Of seedy fields that
The Moon begs The Sun
To harvest,
This eclipse has me wandering
With only my pen,
Searching for even a tease
Of light to record this phenomenon.
My faith goes to you,
My ideal dream, blanket of beauty.
I will find you somehow,
Even collapsed,
I will carry you in the moonlight
Through the sunlight
To a sandy PEI beach,
And music, music, music, music,
Music...a planet of music for you.

Congregate

I want them all to gather in my name,
Suffer for my sins
And weep over how wonderful I am.
In my god-like state,
I will simultaneously penetrate
Piercingly into their defenseless hearts,
A constant reminder that I am above them,
I will feel satisfaction
If I'm allowed.
A well deserved victory
After the loss that broke me.
I will rise above this inferno,
Fire to the incense
Burning on their minds
All mine they are today,
A captivating congregation
All kneeling before me.
I want all of my tears
Multiplied exponentially and
Then uncontrollably.
I want to see Her more than
Anything, my everything,
Flood in her eyes
And holy eternal regret.
My Love,
She created me.

First Snow

Thought crystals float
And settle together,
Each individual pattern
One of infinite traits.
With open arms and
Eyes towards the full white,
This weather has me
Believing once again.
I see it as opportunity
To make four footprints
In a path,
Straight, zig-zagging and falling,
With just enough space in between.
The only thing yet determined
Is which glove will be just right,
In my hands before I venture
Into the winter's sea.
So unregretfully and honestly diving
Into the bank,
Each indentation is a mark
In memory.
First snow,
You are the canvas
To this new chapter painting,
Have I mastered the art
Of my nature yet?

Great Big Sea

Calming blue,
Caress my skin as
I dip in.
I taste your salty tears
And hear the cries
Of your up and down waves.
Let my hands
Nurture your nature
And relieve
Your surface tension.
I sit on the beach
With only a guitar,
Singing your songs,
Hoping they soothe
As well as your
Hypnotic Celtic
Iris ripples.
Great Big Sea,
You create
My favorite island,
A place without
Fears, cares, or horizons.
Strum my soul strings
And reflect the Sun you bring,
Take me to that place
And leave this all behind…

Veil

Thin sweet irish silk,
Caress my blatant heart sleeve,
Only mentally
Can I share
My bed tonight.
Cover me together
And block out
Midnight fear,
A sleep more sound
Could hardly be.
A symbiotic protection
That others may question,
Didn't nature
Intend it this way?
Everything veil,
You comfort me
As you give crave
Of forbidden sleep,
While into our
Eden dream world we go.
Wrapped around
The kindred threads
And unspoken questionables
That make
First star lives
Seem possible tonight…

My Whole World

No poem
Or line
Or phrase
Or word
Or even the smallest period
Could hold
And express
What I wouldn't do
For you...